W0099683

Korea: A Land Divided by War

Laura Santos

Series Editor **Rob Waring**

Level 4- ❾

Korea: A Land Divided by War

Laura Santos

© 2017 Seed Learning, Inc.

Series Editor: Rob Waring
Acquisitions Editor: Liana Robinson
Copy Editor: Casey Malarcher
Cover/Interior Design: Andy Roh

ISBN: 978-1-9464-5240-5

10 9 8 7 6 5 4 3 2 1
21 20 19 18 17

Contents

Two Koreas

There is only one India. There is only one Brazil. There is only one France. Why are there two Koreas?

North Korea and South Korea

The Korean people fought a terrible war from 1950 to 1953. It was not supposed to be a war between different countries. It was supposed to be a civil war: a war between two groups or sides in one country. Those two sides wanted different forms of government for Korea.

The Korean War destroyed the city of Seoul.

A Land Controlled by Other Countries

Long before the Korean War, in 1910, Japan took control of Korea. This made Korea very poor. Then after World War II ended in 1945, the world's most powerful nations were the USSR, or Soviet Union, and the USA.

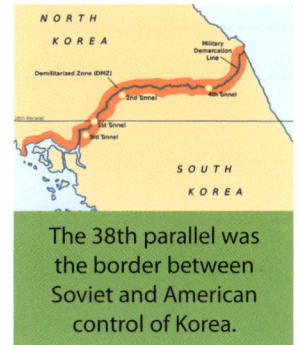

The 38th parallel was the border between Soviet and American control of Korea.

After Japan lost World War II, it no longer controlled Korea. The USSR controlled northern Korea, and the USA controlled southern Korea.

Some Koreans traveled either north or south so they could live under the government that they agreed with. This was difficult in such a poor, damaged country.

Soviet and American sailors enjoying the end of World War II

The Cold War

After World War II, most countries chose to take sides and support either the USSR or the USA. If one country supported the USSR while another country supported the USA, then it was difficult for those two countries to be friends. This developed into the Cold War.

The USSR and the USA had very different politics and economies. The Soviet system was communist. The government owned land and companies and ran them for the benefit of all the people. The USA was a capitalist country where people could own land and companies with very little government control.

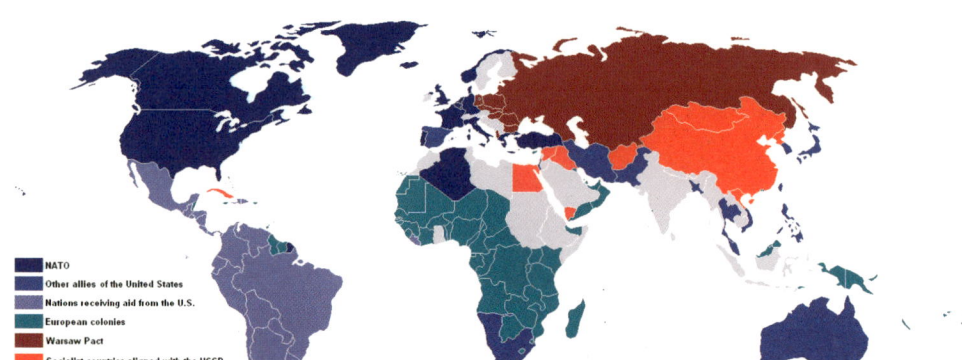

The Cold War divided the world for much of the 20th century.

NATO
Other allies of the United States
Nations receiving aid from the U.S.
European colonies
Warsaw Pact
Socialist countries aligned with the USSR
Other allies of the USSR
Non-aligned nations

The Start of the Korean War

The Soviet army and the American army both left Korea in 1948. However, the two groups of Koreans, both Soviet supporters and American supporters, started a war in June 1950. Each group wanted their form of government to control all of Korea, not just the north or

Kim Il Sung led the North Koreans.

south.

Syngman Rhee, the first president of South Korea

The USSR helped train the North Korean soldiers and gave North Korea tanks, airplanes, guns, and other equipment. Many North Koreans had a strong belief in their government and in the USSR, so they fought very well.

The USSR gave North Korea tanks.

Doubts

The North Korean army was winning. Just 3 days after the war started, North Korea had control of Seoul, the capital of South Korea.

US soldiers came to South Korea in July 1950.

South Korea asked for help. The Americans did not want the USSR supporters to win, so they agreed to help South Korea. Soldiers from 15 other countries, who were members of the United Nations, were also sent to help, but 88% of the foreign soldiers in Korea were American.

In July, the American soldiers arrived in South Korea. Most

North Korea took control of Seoul, the capital of South Korea, in June 1950.

of them were young soldiers without much training. They knew little about Korea. They knew only that the USSR was their enemy, and that the USSR supported North Korea.

US Marines at Busan in 1950

The American soldiers fought alongside the South Korean soldiers. The Americans were surprised by the strength of the attack from North Korea. The Americans were not prepared to meet such a strong enemy.

The South Korean army was not as well-trained as their northern enemies. Their weapons were not as good, either. Plus, South Korea did not have enough soldiers, so the government had to force some men to join the army. It was a very difficult time for South Korea.

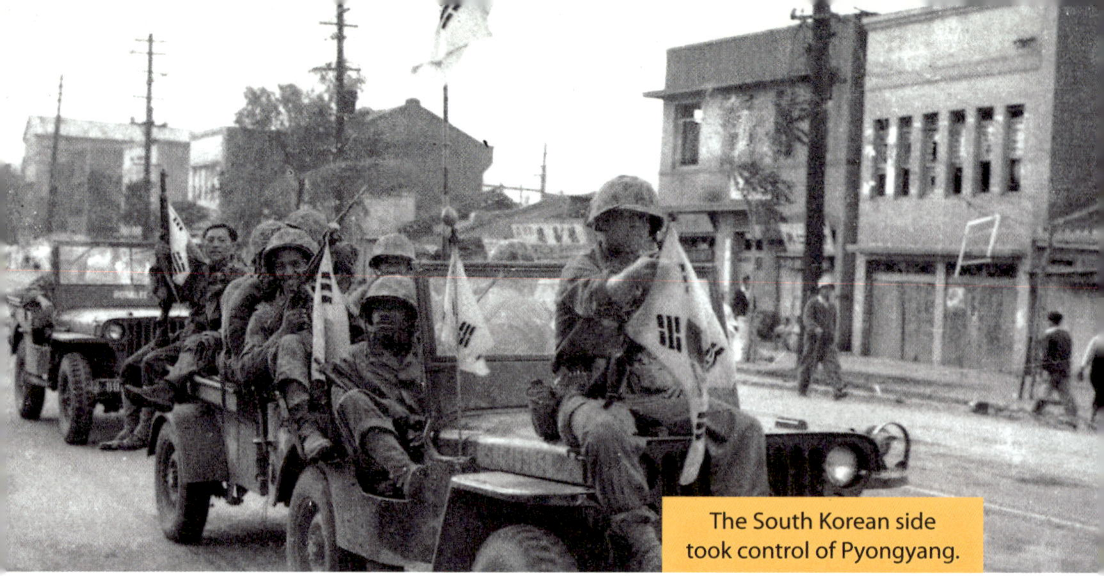

The South Korean side took control of Pyongyang.

North Korea continued to win. By September 1950, the American and South Korean armies controlled only 10% of South Korea. But the USA continued to send soldiers and equipment to South Korea. Slowly, the South Korean side became stronger.

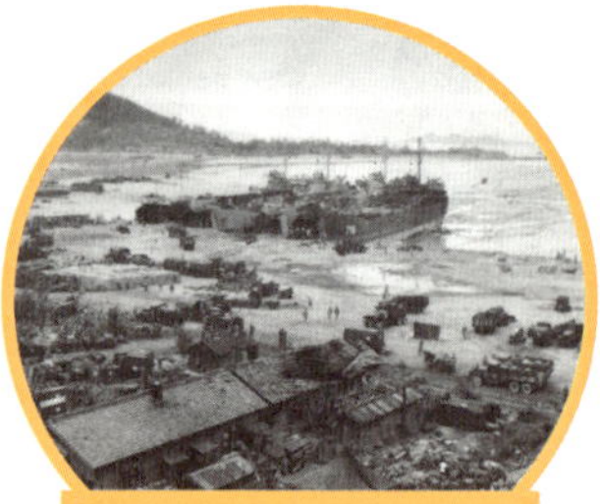

On September 15, General MacArthur landed at Incheon.

In September, US General Douglas MacArthur went by sea to Incheon. This was far behind the North Korean lines, and it surprised them. MacArthur won control of Seoul on September 25, and the North Koreans were pushed back to the north.

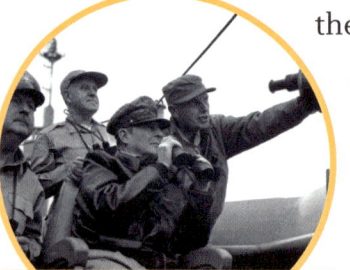

General MacArthur observes the bombing of Incheon.

China in the Korean War

China sent three experienced generals to Korea.

In October 1950, the Chinese government sent soldiers to help North Korea. China wanted to help North Korea because China also supported the USSR.

The Chinese soldiers had a lot of experience at fighting wars. Their army was also very big. Over one million Chinese soldiers fought in the Korean War.

Even though their equipment was not the best, the Chinese soldiers won battles because they had so many more soldiers than the South Koreans. China's huge army could continue the war for many years. By entering the war, China made certain that unifying Korea by force was no longer possible for South Korea and its allies.

Chinese soldiers in Korea

Life During the War

The war was the worst for the ordinary Korean people. Cities were completely destroyed. Hundreds of thousands of people were killed. Often, people left their homes and walked to other towns trying to get away from the fighting.

Looking for coal to try to stay warm

Farmers could not grow food because of the war. Many people died of hunger. It was difficult to find anywhere safe. People got caught in the fighting. They had to move many times in order to get away from the bombs and the soldiers.

Koreans on boats trying to escape the war

Refugees crowd a railway station at Inchon, Korea, 1951.

The crowds of travelers trying to get away from the fighting were confusing and dangerous. Many families got separated and could not find each other. Children lived on the streets with no parents.

Korean refugees, 1952

Everyone was just trying to survive. People were captured or killed. Others starved. Some people drowned trying to cross the Han River. Others froze to death in winter. It was a terrible time.

How Did It End?

By July 1951, both armies knew that no one could win. The fighting countries tried to make an agreement to stop the fighting. It took two years, but an agreement was finally signed in 1953. South Korea did not sign it, but China, North Korea, and the United Nations did.

Usually, when a war ends, we know who won the war. But after all the fighting and killing, Korea was still divided into north and south. The border was still near the 38th parallel. North Korea still supported the USSR, and South Korea still supported the USA.

Bombing the city of Wonsan in North Korea

Military leaders met here to make the agreement.

All South Korean men must serve about 2 years in the military.

Technically, the Korean War never ended. An agreement was made to stop the fighting, but a peace treaty was never signed.

There is still tension between North and South Korea. The border between the two countries is heavily guarded.

All North Korean men must also serve in their military for at least 10 years.

Still Two Koreas

Today, the two Koreas are very different countries. North Korea followed a government like the USSR, but the USSR no longer exists. However, there are still two Koreas.

South Korea is rich and modern, and it is easy for foreigners to visit.

North Korea is poor, and its government does not allow most people to leave or enter the country. Tens of thousands of North Koreans have made the dangerous escape to a better life in South Korea and have told the world how terrible life is in North Korea.

The two Koreas at night

Gangnam, an area in Seoul, the South Korean capital

South Korean soldiers at the border

North and South Korea are enemies. Even today, Korean families that became separated during the war can rarely talk or write to each other.

The two countries still do not trust each other even decades after they stopped fighting. Both sides have many spies. North Korea is one of eight countries that have nuclear weapons. Will they ever use them on their brothers and sisters in South Korea?

Do you think the two Koreas can ever become one country again?

American soldiers at Daegu, South Korea

Comprehension Questions

1. Who controlled Pyongyang before World War II?
   (a) The USSR
   (b) Japan
   (c) The USA
   (d) North Korea

2. Who controlled Seoul from 1945 to 1948?
   (a) The USSR
   (b) Japan
   (c) The USA
   (d) North Korea

3. In June, 1950, the North Korean army was stronger than…
   (a) the South Korean army.
   (b) the Chinese army.
   (c) the Soviet army.
   (d) the Japanese army.

4. Which country was capitalist in 1950?
   (a) The USA
   (b) China
   (c) The USSR
   (d) North Korea

5. Who gave equipment to North Korea?
   (a) The USA
   (b) China
   (c) The USSR
   (d) Japan

6. Who helped South Korea?
   (a) China
   (b) The USA
   (c) The USSR
   (d) North Korea

7. The North Koreans began to lose after…
   (a) China started to fight.
   (b) Japan started to fight.
   (c) the USSR joined the war.
   (d) MacArthur landed at Incheon.

8. The Chinese soldiers won battles because…
   (a) China was richer.
   (b) they had better equipment.
   (c) the Chinese army was big.
   (d) they never fought the Americans.

9. After the fighting stopped, the border between the two Koreas was…
   (a) better for North Korea.
   (b) better for China.
   (c) better for the USSR.
   (d) the same as before the war.

10. Today, North Korea…
    (a) is a poor country.
    (b) does not allow people in.
    (c) does not allow people out.
    (d) All of the above

Key 1. (b) 2. (c) 3. (a) 4. (a) 5. (c) 6. (b) 7. (d) 8. (c) 9. (d) 10. (d)

Glossary

- **alongside** next to; beside

- **army** a group of soldiers fighting a war

- **bomb** something used in war that explodes to damage places or kill people

- **communist** based on the political belief that a country should be highly controlled by the government on behalf of all the people

- **equipment** things that are used for an activity or purpose

- **nuclear weapon** a powerful bomb that uses energy made by dividing the nucleus of an atom to cause an explosion

- **parallel** one of the imaginary circles around the earth that are above or below the equator and never touch the equator

- **soldier** a person who fights for their country

- **Soviet Union** referring to the government of the Union of Soviet Socialist Republics (USSR) from 1922 to 1992

- **spy** a person secretly trying to find out information about another person, country, etc.

- **supporter** a person who agrees with an idea, group, or person

- **tension** a feeling of fear or anger between people or countries

World History Timeline

This chart shows a rough overview of world history.
Some of the dates have been simplified.

World History Timeline

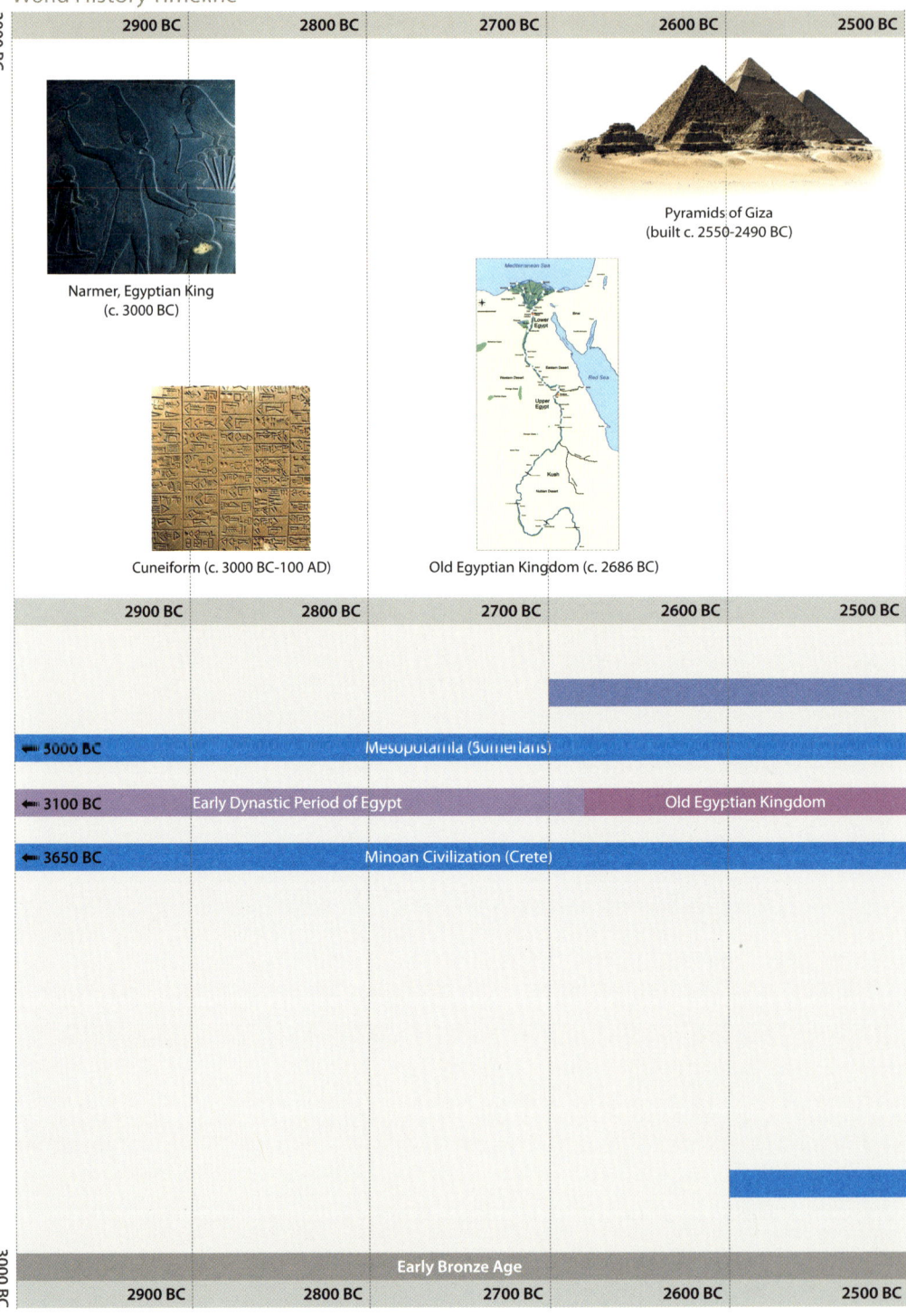

3000 BC	2900 BC	2800 BC	2700 BC	2600 BC	2500 BC

Narmer, Egyptian King
(c. 3000 BC)

Pyramids of Giza
(built c. 2550–2490 BC)

Cuneiform (c. 3000 BC–100 AD)

Old Egyptian Kingdom (c. 2686 BC)

2900 BC	2800 BC	2700 BC	2600 BC	2500 BC

← 5000 BC Mesopotamia (Sumerians)

← 3100 BC Early Dynastic Period of Egypt   Old Egyptian Kingdom

← 3650 BC Minoan Civilization (Crete)

Early Bronze Age

3000 BC	2900 BC	2800 BC	2700 BC	2600 BC	2500 BC

2400 BC	2300 BC	2200 BC	2100 BC	2000 BC

Sahure, Egyptian King
(c. 2487-2475 BC)

Indus Valley
Civilization

Sargon the Great,
Akkadian King
(c. 2340-2284 BC)

Gudea of Lagash
(c. 2144-2124 BC)

Ur III Dynasty (c. 2112-2004 BC)

2400 BC	2300 BC	2200 BC	2100 BC	2000 BC

Xia Dynasty

Gutian Dynasty

Elam (Iran)

Akkadian Empire

Ur III Dynasty

Assyria (Early Period)

Middle Egyptian Kingdom

Minoan Civilization (Crete)

1st Intermediate
Period

Indus Valley Civilization (India)

2400 BC	2300 BC	2200 BC	2100 BC	2000 BC

World History Timeline

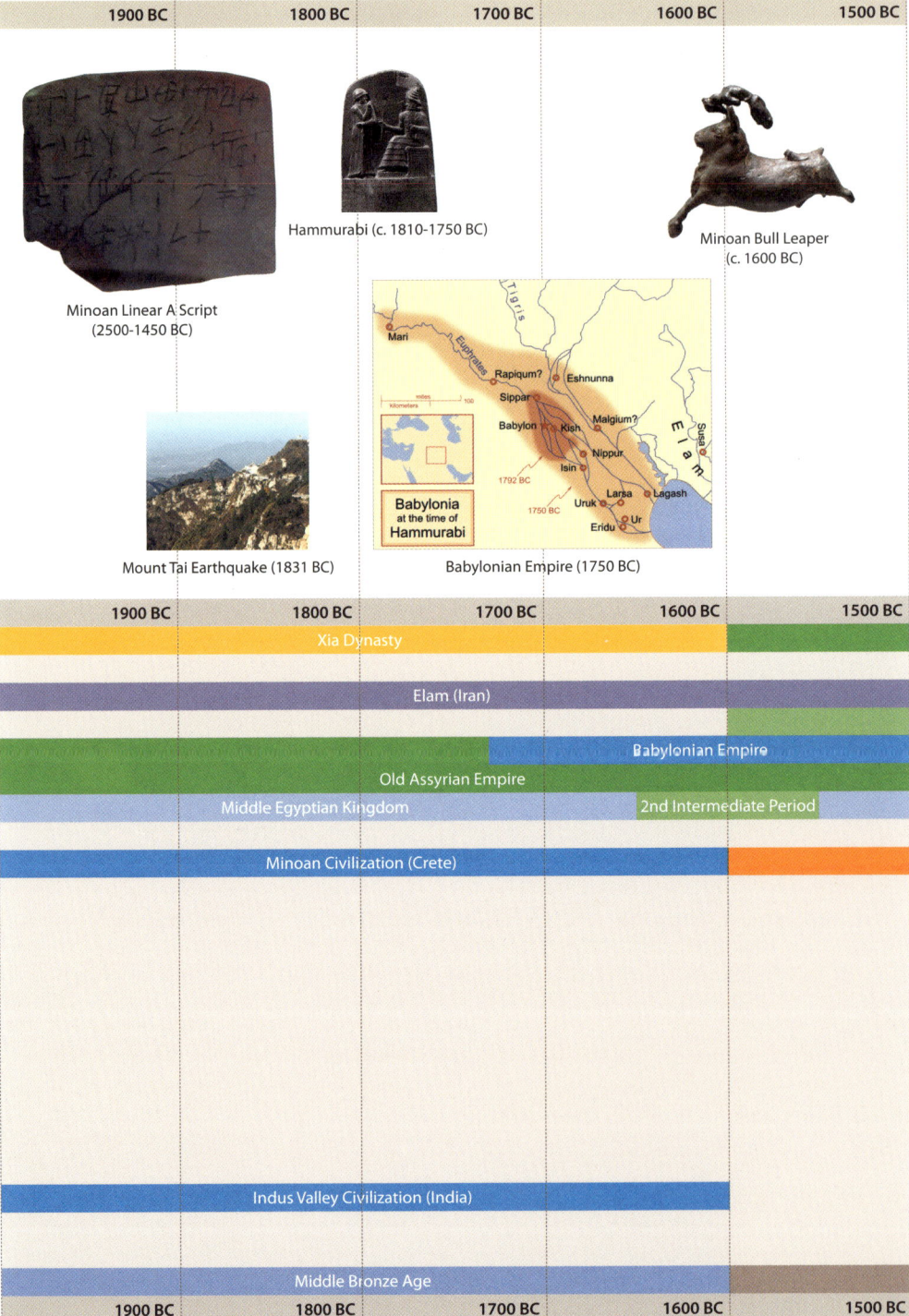

| 1900 BC | 1800 BC | 1700 BC | 1600 BC | 1500 BC |

Hammurabi (c. 1810-1750 BC)

Minoan Bull Leaper
(c. 1600 BC)

Minoan Linear A Script
(2500-1450 BC)

Mount Tai Earthquake (1831 BC)

Babylonian Empire (1750 BC)

| 1900 BC | 1800 BC | 1700 BC | 1600 BC | 1500 BC |

Xia Dynasty

Elam (Iran)

Babylonian Empire

Old Assyrian Empire

Middle Egyptian Kingdom

2nd Intermediate Period

Minoan Civilization (Crete)

Indus Valley Civilization (India)

Middle Bronze Age

| 1900 BC | 1800 BC | 1700 BC | 1600 BC | 1500 BC |

1400 BC	1300 BC	1200 BC	1100 BC	1000 BC

Moses (c. 1391-1271 BC)

Homer

Shang Oracle Bone

Tutankhamun
(ruled c. 1332-1323 BC)

Battle of Kadesh (1274 BC)

Phoenician Alphabet
(c. 1200-150 BC)

1400 BC	1300 BC	1200 BC	1100 BC	1000 BC

Shang Dynasty

Elam (Iran)

Hittites

Neo-Hittites

Middle Assyrian Empire

New Egyptian Kingdom

Mycenaean Greece

Greek Dark Ages

Phoenicia

Olmec Civilization (Mexico)

Vedic Period in India

Late Bronze Age

Early Iron Age

1400 BC	1300 BC	1200 BC	1100 BC	1000 BC

World History Timeline

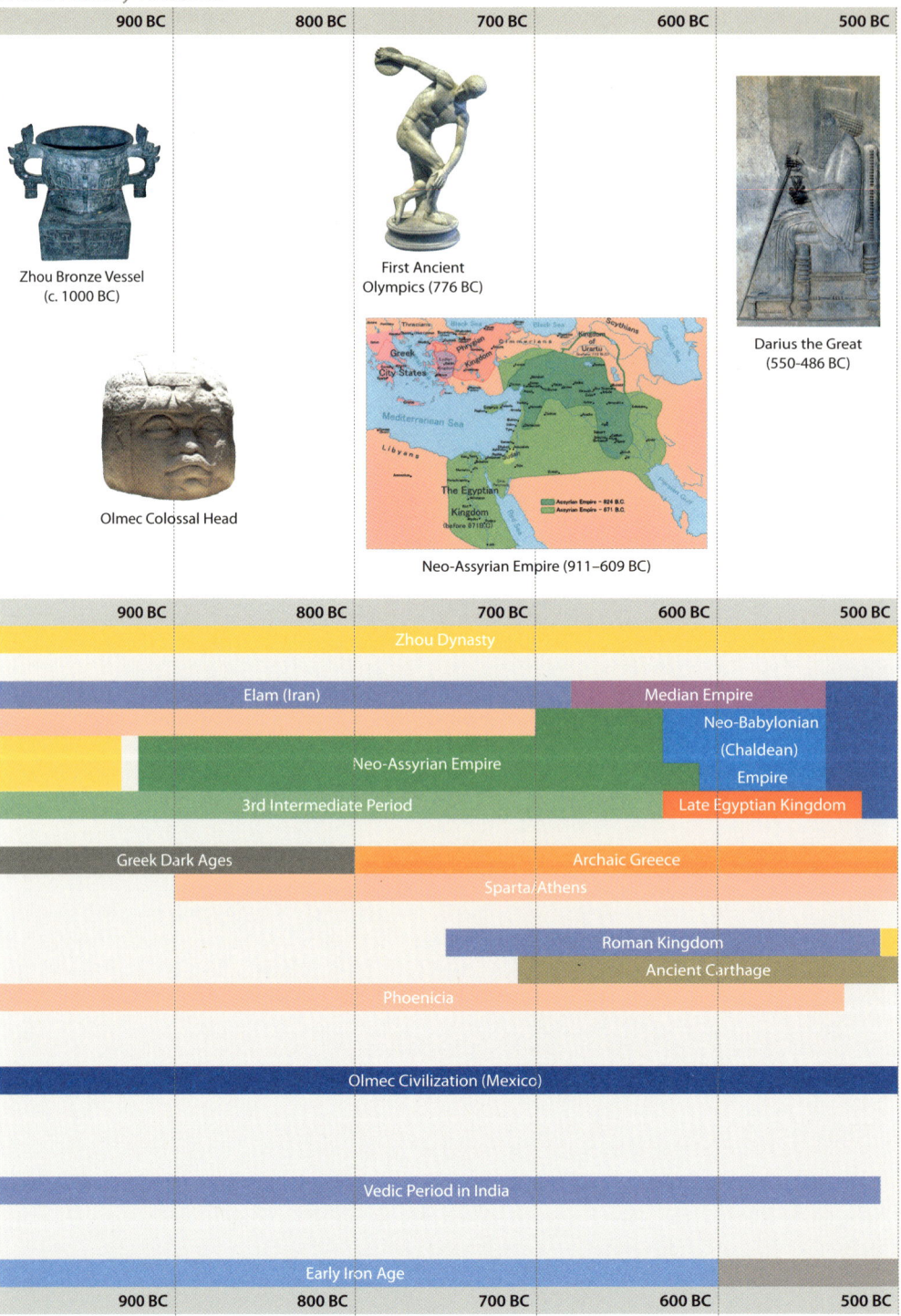

| | 900 BC | 800 BC | 700 BC | 600 BC | 500 BC |

Zhou Bronze Vessel
(c. 1000 BC)

First Ancient
Olympics (776 BC)

Darius the Great
(550-486 BC)

Olmec Colossal Head

Neo-Assyrian Empire (911–609 BC)

| | 900 BC | 800 BC | 700 BC | 600 BC | 500 BC |

Zhou Dynasty

Elam (Iran)

Median Empire

Neo-Babylonian (Chaldean) Empire

Neo-Assyrian Empire

3rd Intermediate Period

Late Egyptian Kingdom

Greek Dark Ages

Archaic Greece

Sparta/Athens

Roman Kingdom

Ancient Carthage

Phoenicia

Olmec Civilization (Mexico)

Vedic Period in India

Early Iron Age

| | 900 BC | 800 BC | 700 BC | 600 BC | 500 BC |

World History Timeline

| 400 BC | 300 BC | 200 BC | 100 BC | 0 |

Alexander the Great
(356-323 BC)

Julius Caesar
(100-44 BC)

Cleopatra
(69-30 BC)

Hannibal
(247-183 BC)

Battle of Salamis
(480 BC)

Seleucid Empire (312-63 BC)

Rossetta Stone
(created 196 BC)

| 400 BC | 300 BC | 200 BC | 100 BC | 0 |

Zhou Dynasty | Qin | Han Dynasty

Achaemenid (Persian) Empire | Alexander the Great | Parthian Empire

Seleucid Empire
Ptolemaic Kingdom
(Hellenistic Greece)

Roman Empire

Classical Greece
Sparta/Athens

Roman Republic | Roman Empire

Maurya Empire

Middle Iron Age

| 400 BC | 300 BC | 200 BC | 100 BC | 0 |

World History Timeline

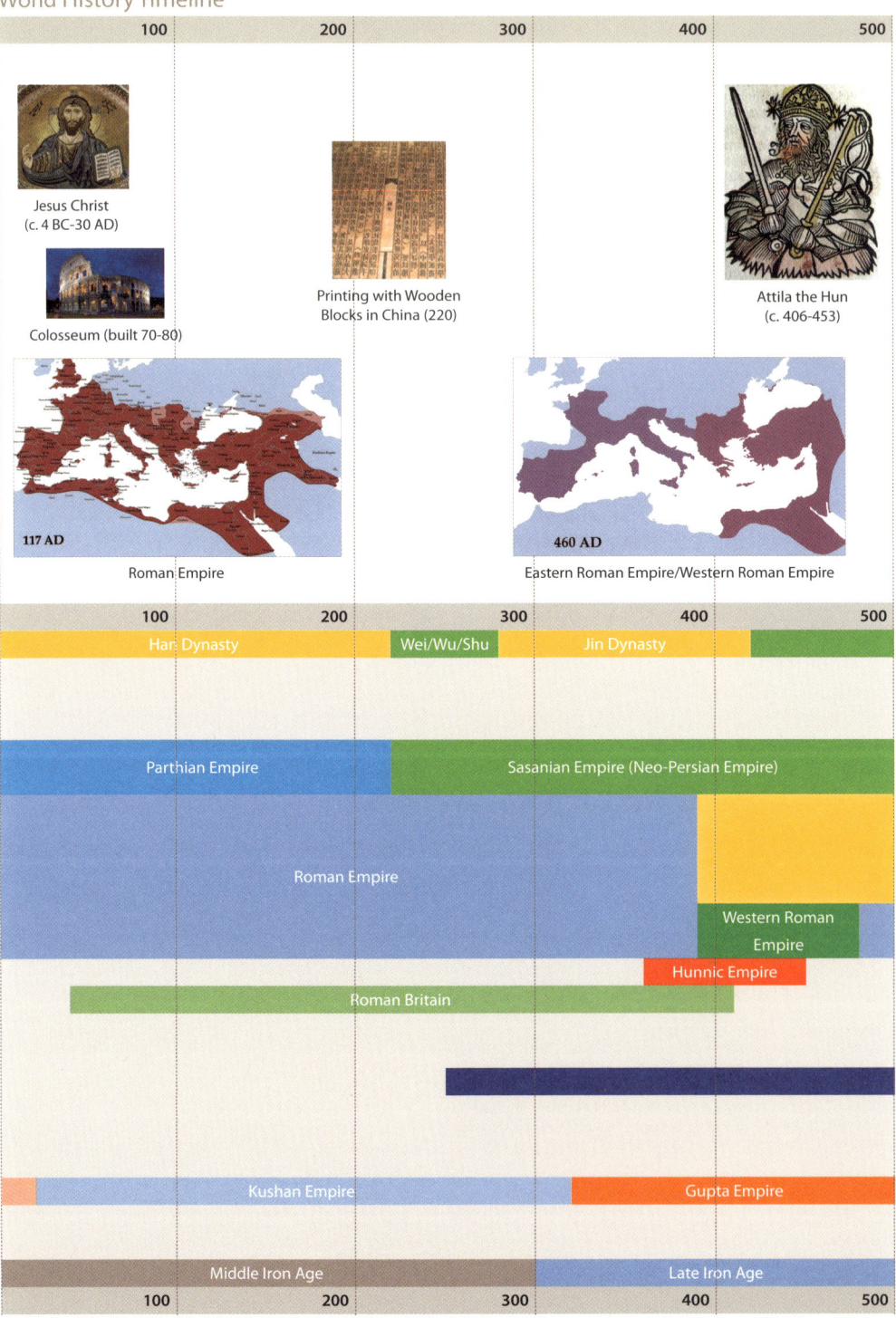

	100	200	300	400	500

Jesus Christ
(c. 4 BC-30 AD)

Colosseum (built 70-80)

Printing with Wooden
Blocks in China (220)

Attila the Hun
(c. 406-453)

117 AD

Roman Empire

460 AD

Eastern Roman Empire/Western Roman Empire

100	200	300	400	500

Han Dynasty · Wei/Wu/Shu · Jin Dynasty

Parthian Empire · Sasanian Empire (Neo-Persian Empire)

Roman Empire

Western Roman Empire

Hunnic Empire

Roman Britain

Kushan Empire · Gupta Empire

Middle Iron Age · Late Iron Age

100	200	300	400	500

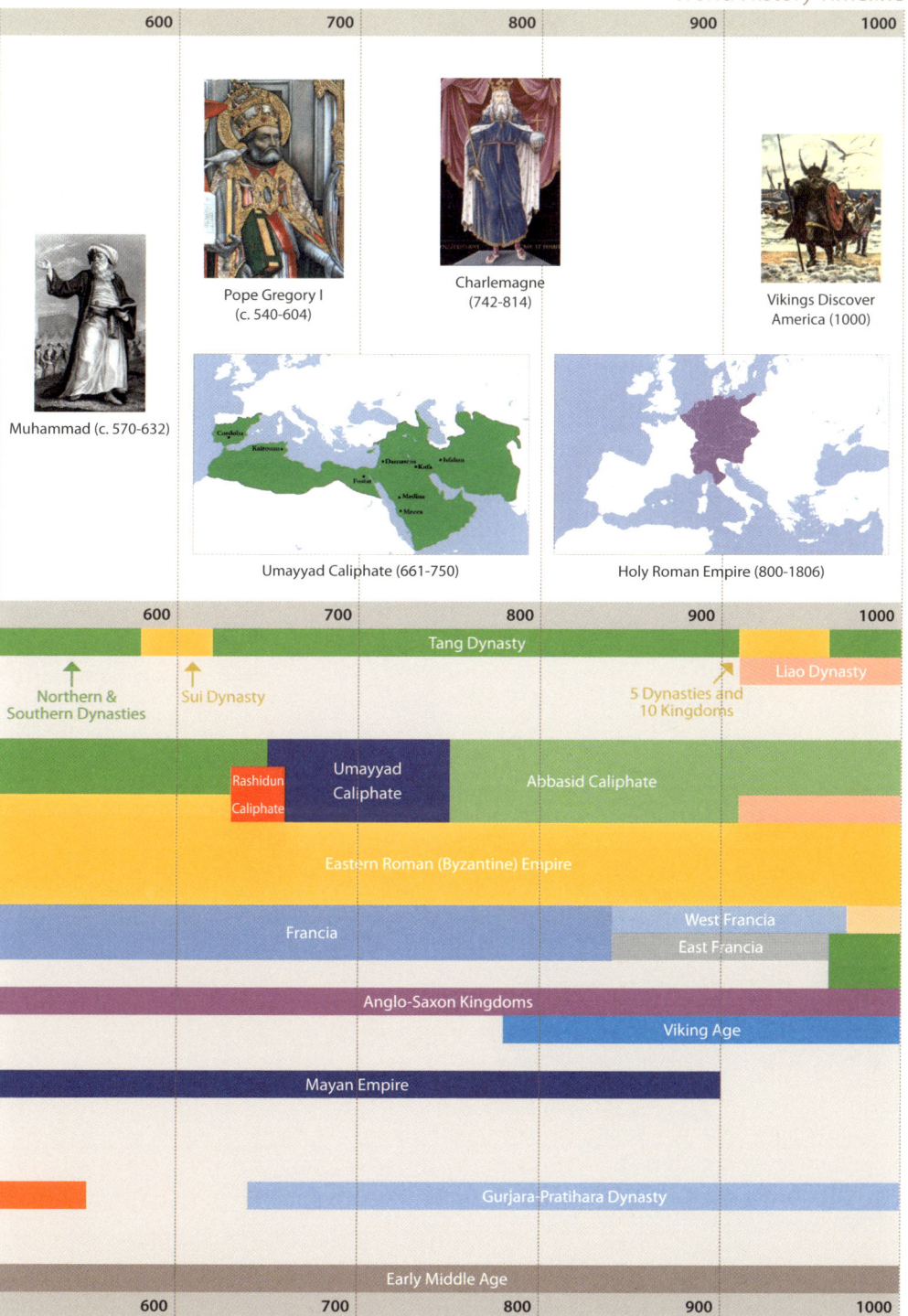

Muhammad (c. 570-632)

Pope Gregory I (c. 540-604)

Charlemagne (742-814)

Vikings Discover America (1000)

Umayyad Caliphate (661-750)

Holy Roman Empire (800-1806)

Tang Dynasty

Sui Dynasty

Northern & Southern Dynasties

Liao Dynasty

5 Dynasties and 10 Kingdoms

Rashidun Caliphate

Umayyad Caliphate

Abbasid Caliphate

Eastern Roman (Byzantine) Empire

Francia

West Francia

East Francia

Anglo-Saxon Kingdoms

Viking Age

Mayan Empire

Gurjara-Pratihara Dynasty

Early Middle Age

World History Timeline

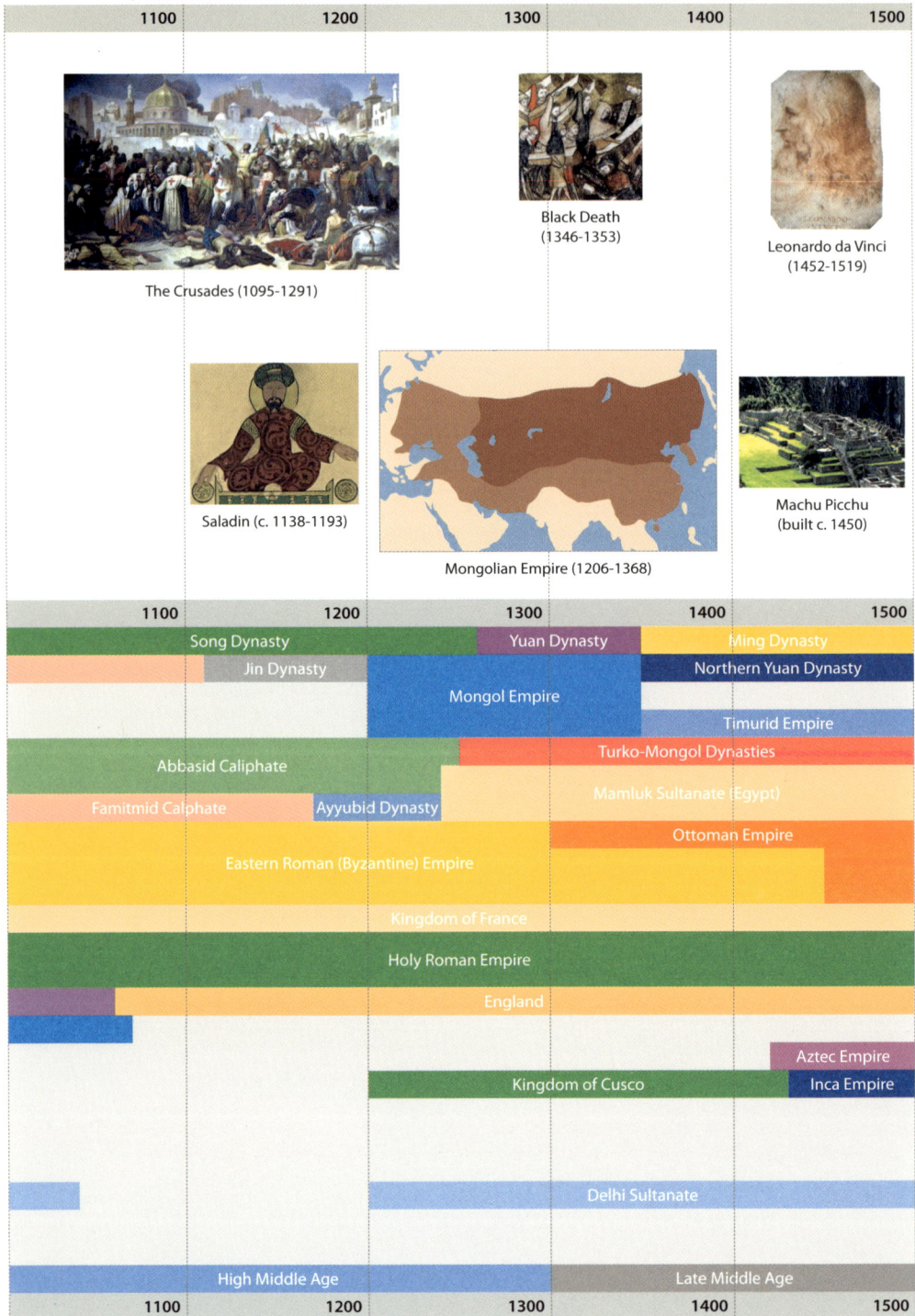

1100	1200	1300	1400	1500

The Crusades (1095-1291)

Black Death (1346-1353)

Leonardo da Vinci (1452-1519)

Saladin (c. 1138-1193)

Mongolian Empire (1206-1368)

Machu Picchu (built c. 1450)

1100	1200	1300	1400	1500

Song Dynasty

Yuan Dynasty

Ming Dynasty

Jin Dynasty

Northern Yuan Dynasty

Mongol Empire

Timurid Empire

Abbasid Caliphate

Turko-Mongol Dynasties

Famitmid Calphate

Ayyubid Dynasty

Mamluk Sultanate (Egypt)

Eastern Roman (Byzantine) Empire

Ottoman Empire

Kingdom of France

Holy Roman Empire

England

Aztec Empire

Kingdom of Cusco

Inca Empire

Delhi Sultanate

High Middle Age

Late Middle Age

1100	1200	1300	1400	1500

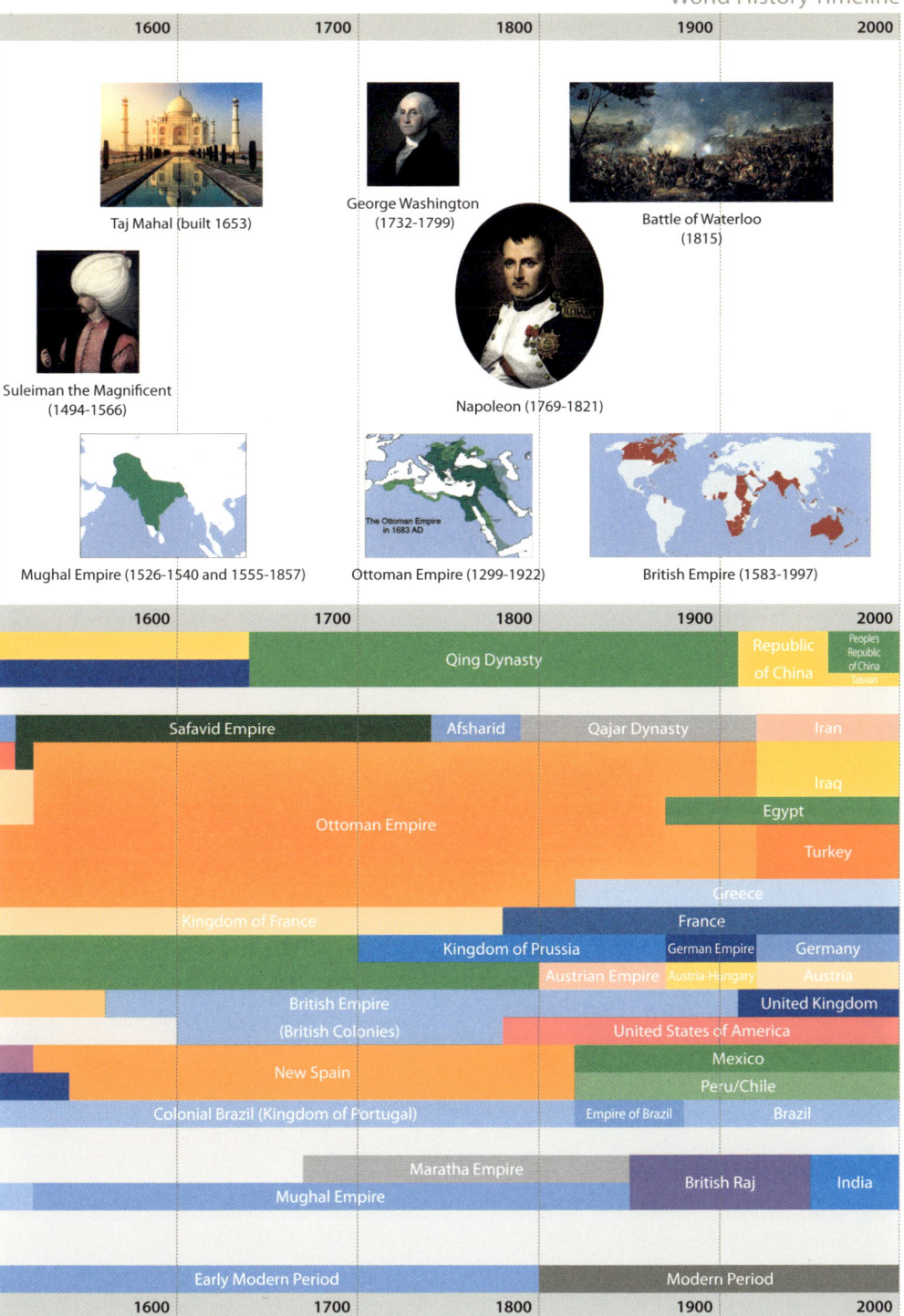

World History Timeline

Taj Mahal (built 1653)

George Washington (1732-1799)

Battle of Waterloo (1815)

Suleiman the Magnificent (1494-1566)

Napoleon (1769-1821)

Mughal Empire (1526-1540 and 1555-1857)

Ottoman Empire (1299-1922)

British Empire (1583-1997)

Qing Dynasty

Republic of China

People's Republic of China / Taiwan

Safavid Empire

Afsharid

Qajar Dynasty

Iran

Ottoman Empire

Iraq

Egypt

Turkey

Greece

Kingdom of France

France

Kingdom of Prussia

German Empire

Germany

Austrian Empire

Austria-Hungary

Austria

British Empire (British Colonies)

United Kingdom

United States of America

New Spain

Mexico

Peru/Chile

Colonial Brazil (Kingdom of Portugal)

Empire of Brazil

Brazil

Maratha Empire

British Raj

India

Mughal Empire

Early Modern Period

Modern Period

List of Books